SWU-800- 016

Das Deutsche Heer des Kaiserreiches zur Jahrhundertwende 1871-1918
band 1

LUCA STEFANO CRISTINI
ILLUSTRATIONEN VON R.KNOTEL

Deutsche & English text

SOLDIERSHOP PUBLISHING

AUTHORS

Richard Knötel (January 12, 1857 – April 26, 1914) was one of the most important German artist and pioneer of the study of military uniform. was born in Glogau in 1857. His father, August Knötel, was an art teacher and gave him lessons in drawing and painting from an early age. In this time, Knötel developed an interest in military fashion and history. By late adolescence, he was already employed as an illustrator for the graphics-based newspaper; Illustrierte Zeitung, as well as for postcards and magazines. In 1880, with an established reputation, Knötel was entered into the Berlin Academy of Fine Arts. After his studies, he began collecting books concerning European military history (it is believed that by his death he owned over 9000 titles), and began work on his most famous piece; Uniformenkunde, a huge collection of plates concerning the armies of Europe from the 17th century to 1914. Uniformenkunde is still perhaps the most widely referenced piece of work the study of military attire of the early modern era, and is still used as a source today. As well as an illustrator, Knötel was a talented painter, who was renowned throughout Germany for his military subjects. He died in Berlin in 1914, and is buried in Saint Matthew's Cemetery in the city.

Luca Stefano Cristini born 21 May 1958 in Bergamo (North Italy) It is the author of several titles in Soldiershop series.

PUBLISHING'S NOTE

None of **unpublished** images or text of our book may be reproduced in any format without the expressed written permission of Soldiershop.com when not indicate as marked with license creative commons 3.0 or 4.0. The publisher remains to disposition of the possible having right for all the doubtful sources images or not identifies. Our trademark: Soldiershop Publishing ©, The names of our series: Soldiers&Weapons, Battlefield, War in colour, PaperSoldiers, Soldiershop e-book etc. are herein © by Soldiershop.com.

NOTE ABOUT BOOK PRINTING BEFORE 1925

This book may contain text or images coming from a reproduction of a book published before 1925 (over seventy years ago). No effort has been made to modernize or standardize the spelling used in the original text, so this book may have occasional imperfections such as missing or blurred pages, poor pictures, errant marks, etc. that were either part of the original artifact, or were introduced by the scanning process. We believe this work is culturally important, and despite the imperfections, have elected to bring it back into print (digital and/or paper) as part of our continuing commitment to the preservation of printed works worldwide. We appreciate your understanding of the imperfections in the preservation process, and hope you enjoy this valuable book. Now this book is purpose re-built and is proof-read and re-type set from the original to provide an outstanding experience of reflowing text, also for an ebook reader. However Soldiershop publishing added, enriched, revised and overhauled the text, images, etc. of the cover and the book. Therefore, the job is now to all intents and purposes a derivative work, and the added, new and original parts of the book are the copyright of Soldiershop. On this second unpublished part of the book none of images or text may be reproduced in any format without the expressed written permission of Soldiershop. Almost many of the images of our books and prints are taken from original first edition prints or books that are no longer in copyright and are therefore public domain. We have been a specialized bookstore for a long time so we (and several friends antiquarian booksellers) have readily available a lot of ancient, historical and illustrated books not in copyright. Each of our prints, art designs or illustrations is either our own creation, or a fully digitally restoration by our computer artists, or non copyrighted images. All of our prints are "tagged" with a registered digital copyright. Soldiershop remains to disposition of the possible having right for all the doubtful sources images or not identifies.

LICENSES COMMONS

This book may utilize material marked with license creative commons 3.0 or 4.0 (CC BY 4.0), (CC BY-ND 4.0), (CC BY-SA 4.0) or (CC0 1.0). We give appropriate attribution credit and indicate if change were made below in the acknowledgements field.

ACKNOWLEDGEMENTS

A Special Thanks to NYPL and other institutions for their kindly permission to use some images of his archives, collections or books used in our book.

Title: DAS DEUTSCHE HEER DES KAISERREICHES ZUR JAHRHUNDERTWENDE 18171-1918 - BAND 1
By Luca S. Cristini. Plates by Richard Knötel. First edition by Soldiershop. April 2020
Cover & Art Design: Luca S. Cristini. ISBN code: 978-88-93275682
Published by Luca Cristini Editore, via Orio 35/4- 24050 Zanica (BG) ITALY. www.soldiershop.com

DAS DEUTSCHE HEER DES KAISERREICHES ZUR JAHRHUNDERTWENDE 1871-1918

BAND 1

GARDEKORPS, I, II UND III ARMEE-KORPS

LUCA STEFANO CRISTINI
ILLUSTRATIONEN VON R. KNÖTEL

*

SWU-800-016

Kronprinz Friedrich Wilhelm von Preußen. Unten rechts auf Weg signiert und datiert Oscar Begas 1867.

DEUTSCHES HEER (DEUTSCHES KAISERREICH)

Deutsches Heer war die offizielle Bezeichnung der Landstreitkräfte des Deutschen Kaiserreiches von 1871 bis 1918. Die Verfassung des Deutschen Reiches verwendet daneben noch den Begriff „Reichsheer" in Anlehnung an das Bundesheer des Norddeutschen Bundes.

Oberbefehlshaber des Deutschen Heeres war der Kaiser. Die Truppenkontingente der deutschen Bundesstaaten standen aufgrund von Militärkonventionen unter preußischem Kommando oder waren ins preußische Heer eingegliedert. Ausnahmen waren die Heere der Königreiche Bayern, Sachsen und Württemberg. Diese Staaten hatten sich beim Beitritt zum Norddeutschen Bund sogenannte Reservatrechte ausgehandelt oder entsprechende Regelungen mit Preußen vereinbart. Das bayerische, sächsische und das württembergische Heer stand im Frieden unter dem Befehl seines jeweiligen Landesherrn. Ihre Verwaltung unterstand eigenen Kriegsministerien. Das sächsische und das württembergische Heer bildeten jeweils ein in sich geschlossenes Armeekorps innerhalb des deutschen Heeres. Das bayerische Heer stellte drei eigene Armeekorps und stand bei der Nummerierung der Truppenteile außerhalb der Zählung des restlichen Heeres. Die Kontingente der kleineren deutschen Staaten bildeten in der Regel geschlossene Verbände innerhalb des preußischen Heeres. Württemberg stellte zu Ausbildungszwecken Offiziere zum preußischen Heer ab. Lediglich Bayern verfügte neben Preußen über eine eigene Kriegsakademie. Die Trennung nach Herkunftsstaaten wurde unter den Notwendigkeiten des Ersten Weltkrieges zwar gelockert, aber nicht aufgegeben.

Der Kaiser hatte auch im Frieden das Recht, die Präsenzstärke festzulegen, die Garnisonen zu bestimmen, Festungen anzulegen und für einheitliche Organisation und Formation, Bewaffnung und Kommando sowie Ausbildung der Mannschaften und Qualifikation der Offiziere zu sorgen. Das Militärbudget wurde durch die Parlamente der einzelnen Bundesstaaten festgelegt. Als Streitkräfte außerhalb des Heeres standen die Schutztruppen der deutschen Kolonien und Schutzgebiete und die Marine einschließlich ihrer drei Seebataillone unter direktem Oberbefehl des Kaisers und der Verwaltung des Reichs.

The Imperial German Army (German: Deutsches Heer) was the unified ground and air force of the German Empire (excluding the maritime aviation formations of the Imperial German Navy). The term Deutsches Heer is also used for the modern German Army, the land component of the Bundeswehr. The German Army was formed after the unification of Germany under Prussian leadership in 1871 and dissolved in 1919, after the defeat of the German Empire in World War I. The states that made up the German Empire contributed their armies; within the German Confederation, formed after the Napoleonic Wars, each state was responsible for maintaining certain units to be put at the disposal of the Confederation in case of conflict. When operating together, the units were known as the Federal Army (Bundesheer). The Federal Army system functioned during various conflicts of the 19th century, such as the First Schleswig War from 1848–50 but by the time of the Second Schleswig War of 1864, tension had grown between the main powers of the confederation, the Austrian Empire and the Kingdom of Prussia and the German Confederation was dissolved after the Austro-Prussian War of 1866. Prussia formed the North German Confederation and the treaty provided for the maintenance of a Federal Army and a Federal Navy (Bundesmarine or Bundeskriegsmarine). Further laws on military duty also used these terms.[2] Conventions (some later amended) were entered into between the North German Confederation and its member states, subordinating their armies to the Prussian army in time of war, and giving the Prussian Army control over training, doctrine and equipment. Shortly after the outbreak of the Franco-Prussian War in 1870, the North German Confederation also entered into conventions on military matters with states that were not members of the confederation, namely Bavaria, Württemberg, and Baden.[b] Through these conventions and the 1871 Constitution of the German Empire, an Army of the Realm (Reichsheer) was created. The contingents of the Bavarian, Saxon and Württemberg kingdoms remained semi-autonomous, while the Prussian Army assumed almost total control over the armies of the other states of the Empire. The Constitution of the German Empire, dated April 16, 1871, changed references in the North German Constitution from Federal Army to either Army of the Realm (Reichsheer) or German Army (Deutsches Heer).

INHALT

*

Deutsches Heer (Deutsches Kaiserreich) 5

Organisation der Deutsches Heer 7

TAFELBAND

Gardekorps (Preussen) 13

I Armee-Korps (Preussen) 37

II Armee-Korps (Preussen) 59

III Armee-Korps (Preussen) 75

ORGANISATION DER DEUTSCHE HEER

In Friedenszeiten war die höchste Führungs-, Ausbildungs- und Verwaltungsebene das Armee-Korps. Die Überwachung aller Maßnahmen der Armee-Korps oblag den Armee-Inspizienten, die in Vertretung des Obersten Kriegsherrn ausschließlich Inspektionsrecht bis in die unterste Ebene, aber keinerlei Führungsaufgaben hatten. Insbesondere bei den jährlichen Manövern traten die Armee-Inspizienten in Erscheinung. Dafür wurde das Heer in Armee-Inspektionen mit zugeteilten Armee-Korps gegliedert. Ursprünglich waren fünf Inspektionen, 1914 dann acht Inspektionen vorhanden. Im Kriegsfall wurden diese Inspektionen in Armeen umgegliedert. Der Stab bestand aus dem Armee-Inspizienten, einem Generalstabsoffizier sowie gegebenenfalls aus einem Adjutanten und einem weiteren Offizier; der Sitz war am jeweiligen Wohnort des Armee-Inspizienten.

Daneben existierten noch die General-Inspektionen und Inspektionen der Waffengattungen. Sie hatten sich um waffengattungsspezifische Angelegenheiten (Ausrüstung, Remontierung etc.) zu kümmern.

INSPEKTION	STANDORT	INSPIZIERTE ARMEEKORPS
I. Armee-Inspektion	Hannover, ab 1900 Berlin, ab 1914 Danzig	1871: I. Armee-Korps, II. Armee-Korps, IX. Armee-Korps, X. Armee-Korps ab 1906: I. Armee-Korps, II. Armee-Korps, IX. Armee-Korps, X. Armee-Korps, XVII. Armee-Korps ab 1914: I. Armee-Korps, II. Armee-Korps, XVII. Armee-Korps
II. Armee-Inspektion	Dresden, ab 1906 Meiningen, ab 1914 Berlin	1871: V. Armee-Korps, VI. Armee-Korps, XII. Armee-Korps ab 1906: V. Armee-Korps, VI. Armee-Korps, XII. Armee-Korps, XIX. Armee-Korps ab 1914: Garde-Korps, XII. (1. Kgl. Sächsisches) Armee-Korps, XIX. (2. Kgl. Sächsisches) Armee-Korps
III. Armee-Inspektion	Darmstadt, ab 1906 Hannover	1871: VII. Armee-Korps, VIII. Armee-Korps, XI. Armee-Korps ab 1906: VII. Armee-Korps, VIII. Armee-Korps, XI. Armee-Korps, XIII. Armee-Korps, XVIII. Armee-Korps ab 1914: IX. Armee-Korps, X. Armee-Korps
IV. Armee-Inspektion	Berlin, ab 1906 München	1871: III. Armee-Korps, IV. Armee-Korps zugeteilt I. Bayerisches Armee-Korps, II. Bayerisches Armee-Korps ab 1906: III. Armee-Korps, IV. Armee-Korps zugeteilt I. Bayerisches Armee-Korps, II. Bayerisches Armee-Korps ab 1914: III. Armee-Korps zugeteilt I. Bayerisches Armee-Korps, II. Bayerisches Armee-Korps, III. Bayerisches Armee-Korps
V. Armee-Inspektion	Karlsruhe	1871: XIV. Armee-Korps, XV. Armee-Korps ab 1906: XIV. Armee-Korps, XV. Armee-Korps, XVI. Armee-Korps ab 1914: IX. Armee-Korps, XIV. Armee-Korps, XV. Armee-Korps
VI. ab 1908 Armee-Inspektion	Stuttgart	IV. Armee-Korps, XI. Armee-Korps, XIII. (Kgl. Württembergisches) Armee-Korps
VII. Ab 1913 Armee-Inspektion	Saarbrücken	XVI. Armee-Korps, XVII. Armee-Korps, XXI. Armee-Korps
VIII. Ab 1914 Armee-Inspektion	Berlin	XI. Armee-Korps, XVIII. Armee-Korps, XX. Armee-Korps

Daneben bestand ab 1898 die Generalinspektion der Kavallerie, der die Kavalleriebrigaden der Divisionen jedoch nicht unterstellt waren:
Generalinspektion der Kavallerie in Berlin
1. Kavallerie-Inspektion   in Königsberg
2. Kavallerie-Inspektion   in Stettin
3. Kavallerie-Inspektion   in Münster
4. Kavallerie-Inspektion   in Saarbrücken, 1900/02 in Potsdam

Den 25 Armeekorps, davon drei bayerische mit separater Nummerierung, zwei sächsische und ein württembergisches, unterstanden in der Regel zwei Divisionen. Die Gesamtstärke eines Armeekorps betrug 1554 Offiziere, 43.317 Mann, 16.934 Pferde und 2933 Fahrzeuge.

Die Divisionen umfassten in der Regel zwei Infanteriebrigaden zu je zwei Regimentern, eine Kavalleriebrigade zu zwei Kavallerie-Regimentern und eine Feldartilleriebrigade zu zwei Regimentern. Ein Infanterie-Regiment bestand normalerweise aus drei Bataillonen zu je vier Kompanien, pro Regiment also zwölf Kompanien. Die Aufrüstung der Jahre 1912/1913 brachte für nahezu alle Regimenter die Aufstellung einer 13. (Maschinengewehr-)Kompanie. Ein Kavallerie-Regiment bestand aus fünf Eskadronen, in Bayern zum Teil nur aus vier Eskadronen. Daneben standen einem Armeekorps als Korpstruppen ein bis zwei Fußartillerieregimenter, ein Jägerbataillon, ein bis zwei Pionierbataillone, ein Trainbataillon sowie teilweise verschiedene weitere Verbände, wie beispielsweise ein Telegraphenbataillon, ein bis zwei Feldpionierkompanien, ein bis zwei Sanitätskompanien, Eisenbahnkompanien usw. zur Verfügung.

Ein Infanterieregiment hatte 1900 eine Friedensstärke von 69 Offizieren, 6 Ärzten, 1977 Unteroffizieren und Mannschaften sowie 6 Militärbeamten, insgesamt also 2058 Mann. Ein Kavallerieregiment kam auf 760 Mann und 702 Dienstpferde. Diese Stärke galt für Regimenter mit hohem Etat. Regimenter mit mittlerem oder niedrigerem Etat hatten eine geringere Stärke. Eine Infanteriekompanie mit hohem Etat hatte 5 Offiziere und 159 Unteroffiziere und Mannschaften, mit niedrigerem Etat 4 Offiziere und 141 Unteroffiziere und Mannschaften. Bei der Kavallerie bestanden im Frieden keine Korps, nur eine Division, die Garde-Kavallerie-Division. Bei der Mobilmachung zum Ersten Weltkrieg wurde die Kavallerie aufgeteilt in Heereskavallerie und Divisionskavallerie.

DAS REICHSHEER UMFASSTE 1914:

Stäbe
25 Generalkommandos
50 Infanteriedivisionen und 1 Kavalleriedivision
25 Landwehrinspektionen
106 Infanterie-, 55 Kavallerie-, 50 Feldartillerie-, 7 Fußartillerie- und 2 Eisenbahn-Brigaden

Infanterie
651 Infanteriebataillone in 217 Regimentern zu je drei Bataillonen
18 Jäger- und Schützenbataillone
233 MG-Kompanien, je eine für jedes Infanterieregiment und für 16 Jägerbataillone
11 MG-Abteilungen für die bei Mobilisierung zu bildenden Kavalleriedivisionen
15 Festungs-MG-Abteilungen
9 Unteroffiziersschulen, 1 Lehr-Infanteriebataillon, 1 Infanterie-Schießschule, 1 Gewehr-Prüfungskommission

Kavallerie
547 Kavallerieeskadronen in 107 Regimentern zu je fünf und 3 Regimentern zu je vier Eskadronen

Artillerie
600 fahrende und 33 reitende Feldartilleriebatterien in 100 Regimentern zu je zwei oder drei Abteilungen
1 Lehr-Feldartillerieregiment der Feldartillerie-Schießschule
190 Fußartilleriebatterien in 24 Regimentern zu je zwei Bataillonen
30 Bespannungsabteilungen der Fußartillerie
1 Lehr-Fußartillerieregiment der Fußartillerieschießschule

Pioniere
35 Pionierbataillone mit 26 Scheinwerferzügen
9 Kommandos der Pioniere für je zwei unterstellte Pionierbataillone

Verkehrstruppen
8 Eisenbahnbataillone, 6 davon in 3 Regimentern zu je zwei Bataillonen, 2 selbstständig

9 Telegrafenbataillone

8 Festungs-Fernsprechkompanien

5 Luftschifferbataillone

5 Fliegerbataillone

1 Kraftfahrbataillon

1 (bayerisches) Luft- und Kraftfahrbataillon

Train
25 Trainabteilungen

außerdem

317 Bezirkskommandos

Entwicklung der Mannstärke des deutschen Heeres zu ausgewählten Zeitpunkten:

Jahr	1875	1888	1891	1893	1899	1902	1906	1808	1911	1913	1914
Soldaten	420.000	487.000	507.000	580.000	591.000	605.000	610.000	613.000	617.000	663.000	794.000

Truppengattungen
Neben den bisherigen klassischen Truppengattungen Infanterie, Kavallerie und Artillerie entstanden auf Grund der technischen Entwicklungen neue Truppengattungen, teilweise durch die Vergrößerung schon früher bestehender kleinerer Einheiten (Pioniere, Train), teilweise durch die Verwendung neuer technischer Geräte und Anwendungen durch die Armee.

ARMY STRUCTURE (ENGLISH)

The Kaiser had full control of the armed forces, but used a highly complex organizational structure. The basic peacetime organizational structure of the Imperial German Army were the Army inspectorate (Armee-Inspektion), the army corps (Armeekorps), the division and the regiment. During wartime, the staff of the Army inspectorates formed field army commands, which controlled the corps and subordinate units. During World War I, a higher command level, the army group (Heeresgruppe), was created. Each army group controlled several field armies.

Army inspectorate
Germany was divided into army inspectorates, each of which oversaw three or four corps. There were five in 1871, with three more added between 1907 and 1913.

I Army Inspectorate: Headquartered in Danzig, became the 8th Army on mobilisation (2 August 1914)

II Army Inspectorate: Headquartered in Berlin, became the 3rd Army on mobilisation (2 August 1914)

III Army Inspectorate: Headquartered in Hannover, became the 2nd Army on mobilisation (2 August 1914)

IV Army Inspectorate: Headquartered in Munich, became the 6th Army on mobilisation (2 August 1914)

V Army Inspectorate: Headquartered in Karlsruhe, became the 7th Army on mobilisation (2 August 1914)

VI Army Inspectorate: Headquartered in Stuttgart, became the 4th Army on mobilisation (2 August 1914)

VII Army Inspectorate: Headquartered in Berlin, became the 5th Army on mobilisation (2 August 1914)

VIII Army Inspectorate: Headquartered in Saarbrücken, became the 1st Army on mobilisation (2 August 1914)

Corps
The basic organizational formation was the army corps (Armeekorps). The corps consisted of two or more divisions and various support troops, covering a geographical area. The corps was also responsible for maintaining the reserves and Landwehr in the corps area. By 1914, there were 21 corps areas under Prussian jurisdiction and three Bavarian army corps. Besides the regional corps, there was also a Guard Corps (Gardecorps), which controlled the elite Prussian Guard units. A corps usually included a light infantry (Jäger) battalion, a heavy artillery (Fußartillerie) battalion, an engineer

battalion, a telegraph battalion and a trains battalion. Some corps areas also disposed of fortress troops; each of the 25 corps had a Field Aviation Unit (Feldflieger Abteilung) attached to it normally equipped with six unarmed „A" or „B" class unarmed two-seat observation aircraft apiece.

In wartime, the army corps became a mobile tactical formation and four Höhere Kavallerie-Kommando (Higher Cavalry Commands) were formed from the Cavalry Inspectorate, the equivalent of corps, being made up of two divisions of cavalry.

The areas formerly covered by the corps each became the responsibility of a Wehrkreis (Military District, sometimes translated as Corps Area). The Military Districts were to supervise the training and enlistment of reservists and new recruits. Originally each Military District was linked to an army corps; thus Wehrkreis I took over the area that I. Armeekorps had been responsible for and sent replacements to the same formation. The first sixteen Reserve Corps raised followed the same pattern; X. Reserve-Korps was made up of reservists from the same area as X. Armeekorps. However, these links between rear areas and front line units were broken as the war went on and later corps were raised with troops from all over Germany.

Division

The basic tactical formation was the division. A standard Imperial German division consisted of two infantry brigades of two regiments each, a cavalry brigade of two regiments, and an artillery brigade of two regiments. One of the divisions in a corps area usually also managed the corps Landwehr region (Landwehrbezirk). In 1914, besides the Guard Corps (two Guard divisions and a Guard cavalry division), there were 42 regular divisions in the Prussian Army (including four Saxon divisions and two Württemberg divisions), and six divisions in the Bavarian Army.

These divisions were all mobilized in August 1914. They were reorganized, receiving engineer companies and other support units from their corps, and giving up most of their cavalry to form cavalry divisions. Reserve divisions were also formed, Landwehr brigades were aggregated into divisions, and other divisions were formed from replacement (Ersatz) units. As World War I progressed, additional divisions were formed, and by wars' end, 251 divisions had been formed or reformed in the German Army's structure.

Regiment

The regiment was the basic combat unit as well as the recruiting base for soldiers. When inducted, a soldier entered a regiment, usually through its replacement battalion, and received his basic training. There were three basic types of regiment: infantry, cavalry and artillery. Other specialties, such as pioneers (combat engineers) and signal troops, were organized into smaller support units. Regiments also carried the traditions of the army, in many cases stretching back into the 17th and 18th centuries. After World War I, regimental traditions were carried forward in the Reichswehr and its successor, the Wehrmacht, but the chain of tradition was broken in 1945 as West German and East German units did not carry forward pre-1945 traditions.

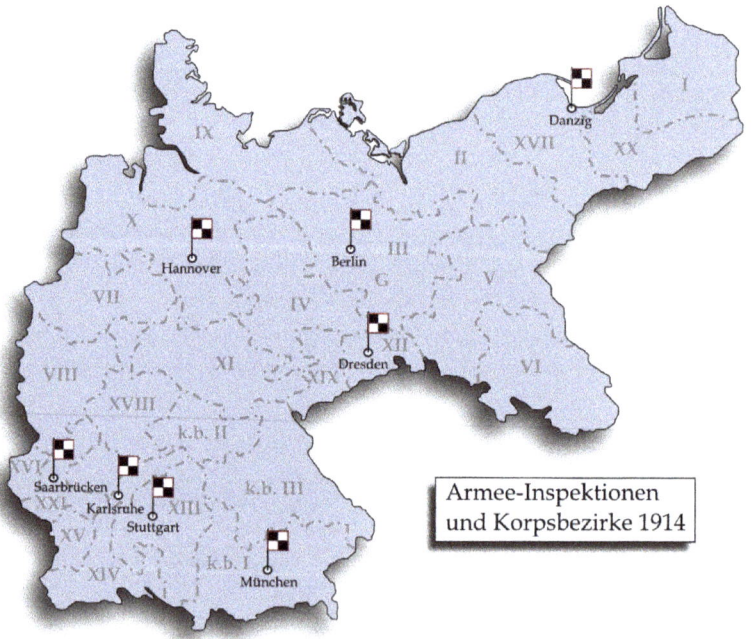

Armee-Inspektionen und Korpsbezirke 1914

National contingents

The German Empire was formed by 38

duchies and kingdoms each with their traditions of warfare. Although the new army of the united German Empire was nominally „German", it was formed from separate national contingents which behaved autonomously:

The Royal Saxon Army...was the national army of the Kingdom of Saxony one of the four states of the German Reich to retain its own armed forces.

Nevertheless, in times of war, all of these would pledge allegiance to the Kaiser and the German nation. They did however remain organizationally distinct, being able to raise units of their own without assistance from the dominating Prussians. In one instance, Freiherr von Sonden (from Württemberg) was able to „quite legitimately send a request directly to the Ministry of War in Stuttgart for the raising of a new artillery regiment".

Regiments and units from separate constituents were also raised locally and often numbered independently from each other - for example, there was (among others) both a Bavarian 1st Infantry Regiment and a Württemberger 1st Infantry Regiment

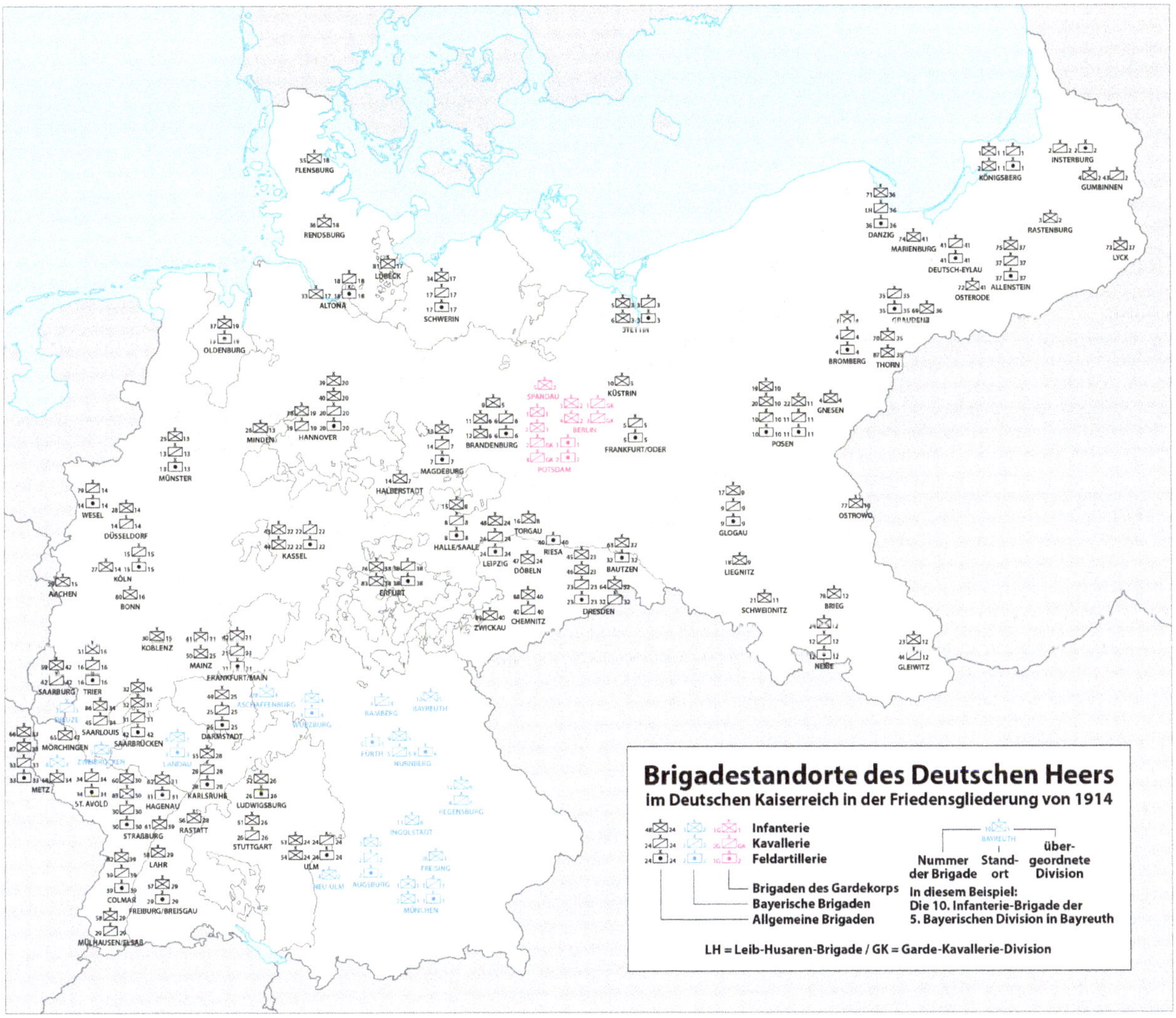

Richard Knötel (1857 in Glogau; 1914 in Berlin) war ein deutscher Maler, Lithograf und Schriftsteller. Er gilt als einer der bedeutendsten deutschen Historienmaler. Knötel war der Sohn des Oberlehrers, Malers und Schriftstellers Augustin Knötel.

Er erhielt von seinem Vater Zeichenunterricht, studierte seit 1880 an der Berliner Akademie der bildenden Künste und beschäftigte sich eingehend mit der Geschichte des Militärs.

Im Jahr 1888 zeichnete er für das Militärbilderbuch Die Kriegsheere Europas, welches von Oberstleutnant a. d. Vogt beschrieben wurde. Er war eines der Gründungsmitglieder der Deutschen Gesellschaft für Heereskunde e. V. Richard Knötel wurde auf dem St. Matthias-Friedhof in Berlin-Tempelhof beigesetzt. Sein Sohn Herbert wurde ebenfalls Maler und errang sich einen Namen als „Knötel, der Jüngere".

GARDEKORPS (PREUSSEN)

1. Garde-Division in Potsdam, Berlin
2. Garde-Division in Berlin
Garde-Kavallerie- Division in Berlin
Garde-Fußartillerie-Regiment in Spandau
Garde-Train-Abteilung in Berlin
Garde-Pionier-Bataillon in Berlin

1 Garde-Division

1. Garde-Infanterie-Brigade in Potsdam
  1. Garde-Regiment zu Fuß in Potsdam
  3. Garde-Regiment zu Fuß in Potsdam
  Garde-Jäger-Bataillon in Potsdam

2. Garde-Infanterie-Brigade in Potsdam
  2. Garde-Regiment zu Fuß in Berlin
  Garde-Füsilier-Regiment in Berlin
  4. Garde-Regiment zu Fuß in Berlin

2 Garde-Division

3. Garde-Infanterie-Brigade in Berlin
  Kaiser Alexander Garde-Grenadier-Regiment Nr. 1 in Berlin
  Königin Elisabeth Garde-Grenadier-Regiment Nr. 3 in Charlottenburg
  Garde-Schützen-Bataillon in Lichterfelde

4. Garde-Infanterie-Brigade in Berlin
  Kaiser Franz Garde-Grenadier-Regiment Nr. 2 in Berlin
  Königin Augusta Garde-Grenadier-Regiment Nr. 4 in Berlin

5. Garde-Infanterie-Brigade in Spandau
  5. Garde-Regiment zu Fuß in Spandau
  Garde-Grenadier-Regiment Nr. 5 in Spandau

Garde-Kavallerie-Division

1. Garde-Kavallerie-Brigade in Berlin
  Regiment der Gardes du Corps in Potsdam
  Garde-Kürassier-Regiment in Berlin

2. Garde-Kavallerie-Brigade in Potsdam
  1. Garde-Ulanen-Regiment in Potsdam
  3. Garde-Ulanen-Regiment in Potsdam

3. Garde-Kavallerie-Brigade in Berlin
  1. Garde-Dragoner-Regiment „Königin Viktoria von Großbritannien und Irland" in Berlin
  2. Garde-Dragoner-Regiment „Kaiserin Alexandra von Rußland" in Berlin

4. Garde-Kavallerie-Brigade in Potsdam
  Leib-Garde-Husaren-Regiment in Potsdam
  2. Garde-Ulanen-Regiment in Potsdam

An das Armeekorps angeschlossen

  Garde-Fußartillerie-Regiment in Spandau
  Garde-Train-Abteilung in Berlin
  Garde-Pionier-Bataillon in Berlin

1. Garde-Division 1. Garde-Infanterie-Brigade 1. Garde-Regiment zu Fuß in Potsdam

1. Garde-Division 1. Garde-Infanterie-Brigade 3. Garde-Regiment zu Fuß in Potsdam

1. Garde-Division 1. Garde-Infanterie-Brigade Garde-Jäger-Bataillon in Potsdam

1. Garde-Division 2. Garde-Infanterie-Brigade 2. Garde-Regiment zu Fuß in Berlin

2.Garde-Division 3.Garde-Infanterie-Brigade Kaiser Alexander Garde-Grenadier-Regiment Nr. 1 in Berlin

2.Garde-Division 3.Garde-Infanterie-Brigade Königin Elisabeth Garde-Grenadier-Regiment Nr. 3 in Charlottenburg

2. Garde-Division 3. Garde-Infanterie-Brigade Garde-Schützen-Bataillon in Lichterfelde

2.Garde-Division 4.Garde-Infanterie-Brigade Kaiser Franz Garde-Grenadier-Regiment Nr. 2 in Berlin

2.Garde-Division 4. Garde-Infanterie-Brigade Königin Augusta Garde-Grenadier-Regiment Nr. 4 in Berlin

2.Garde-Division 5.Garde-Infanterie-Brigade 5.Garde-Regiment zu Fuß in Spandau

2.Garde-Division 5.Garde-Infanterie-Brigade Garde-Grenadier-Regiment Nr. 5 in Spandau

Garde-Kavallerie Division 1. Garde-Kavallerie-Brigade Regiment der Gardes du Corps in Potsdam

Garde-Kavallerie Division 1. Garde-Kavallerie-Brigade Garde-Kürassier-Regiment in Berlin

Garde-Kavallerie Division 2. Garde-Kavallerie-Brigade 1. Garde-Ulanen-Regiment in Potsdam

Garde-Kavallerie Division 1. Garde-Kavallerie-Brigade 3. Garde-Ulanen-Regiment in Potsdam

Garde-Kavallerie Division 3.Garde-Kavallerie-Brigade 1.Garde-Dragoner-Regiment „Königin Viktoria von Großbritannien und Irland" in Berlin

Garde-Kavallerie Division 3.Garde-Kavallerie-Brigade 2. Garde-Dragoner-Regiment „Kaiserin Alexandra von Rußland" in Berlin

Garde-Kavallerie Division 4. Garde-Kavallerie-Brigade Leib-Garde-Husaren-Regiment in Potsdam

Garde-Kavallerie Division 4. Garde-Kavallerie-Brigade 2. Garde-Ulanen-Regiment in Potsdam

Garde-Pionier-Bataillon in Berlin

1. Garde-Fußartillerie-Regiment in Spandau

2. Garde-Fußartillerie-Regiment in Spandau

Garde-Train-Abteilung in Berlin

I ARMEE-KORPS (PREUSSEN)

1. Division in Königsberg
2. Division in Insterburg
37. Division in Allenstein
Jäger-Bataillon „Graf Yorck von Wartenberg" (Ostpreußisches) Nr. 1
Eskadron Jäger zu Pferde des I. Armee-Korps (beim Kürassier-Regiment „Graf Wrangel" (Ostpreußisches) Nr. 3)
Fußartillerie-Regiment „von Linger" (Ostpreußisches) Nr. 1
Pionier-Bataillon „Fürst Radziwill" (Ostpreußisches) Nr. 1
Pionier-Bataillon Nr. 18
Ostpreußisches Train-Bataillon Nr. 1
11 Landwehrbezirkskommandos

1 division
1. Infanterie-Brigade in Tilsit
  Grenadier-Regiment „Kronprinz" (1. Ostpreußisches) Nr. 1 in Königsberg
  Infanterie-Regiment „von Boyen" (5. Ostpreußisches) Nr. 41 in Tilsit und Memel (III. Bataillon)
2. Infanterie-Brigade in Königsberg
  Grenadier-Regiment „König Friedrich Wilhelm I." (2. Ostpreußisches) Nr. 3 in Königsberg
  Infanterie-Regiment „Herzog Karl von Mecklenburg-Strelitz" (6. Ostpreußisches) Nr. 43 in Königsberg und Pillau (II. Bataillon)
1. Kavallerie-Brigade in Königsberg
  Kürassier-Regiment „Graf Wrangel" (Ostpreußisches) Nr. 3 in Königsberg
  Dragoner-Regiment „Prinz Albrecht von Preußen" (Litthauisches) Nr. 1 in Tilsit
1. Feldartillerie-Brigade in Königsberg
  1. Ostpreußisches Feldartillerie-Regiment Nr. 16 in Königsberg
  2. Ostpreußisches Feldartillerie-Regiment Nr. 52 in Königsberg

2 division
3. Infanterie-Brigade in Rastenburg
  Grenadier-Regiment „König Friedrich der Große" (3. Ostpreußisches) Nr. 4 in Rastenburg
  Infanterie-Regiment „Graf Dönhoff" (7. Ostpreußisches) Nr. 44 in Goldap
4. Infanterie-Brigade in Gumbinnen
  Füsilier-Regiment „Graf Roon" (Ostpreußisches) Nr. 33 in Gumbinnen
  8. Ostpreußisches Infanterie-Regiment Nr. 45 in Insterburg und Darkehmen (I. Bataillon)
2. Kavallerie-Brigade in Insterburg
  Litthauisches Ulanen-Regiment Nr. 12 in Insterburg
  Jäger-Regiment zu Pferde Nr. 9 in Insterburg
43. Kavallerie-Brigade in Gumbinnen und Stallupönen (1. und 3. Eskadron)
  Ulanen-Regiment „Graf zu Dohna" (Ostpreußisches) Nr. 8 in Gumbinnen
  Jäger-Regiment zu Pferde Nr. 10 in Angerburg und Goldap (1. Eskadron)
2. Feldartillerie-Brigade in Insterburg
  Feldartillerie-Regiment „Prinz August von Preußen" (1. Litthauisches) Nr. 1 in Gumbinnen und Insterburg (I. Abteilung)
  2. Litthauisches Feldartillerie-Regiment Nr. 37 in Insterburg

37 division

1.Division 1.Infanterie-Brigade Grenadier-Regiment „Kronprinz" (1. Ostpreußisches) Nr. 1 in Königsberg

1.Division 2.Infanterie-Brigade Grenadier-Regiment „König Friedrich Wilhelm I." (2. Ostpreußisches) Nr. 3 in Königsberg

1 Division 1 Kavallerie-Brigade Kürassier-Regiment „Graf Wrangel" (Ostpreußisches) Nr. 3 in Königsberg

1.Division 1.Kavallerie-Brigade Dragoner-Regiment „Prinz Albrecht von Preußen" (Litthauisches) Nr. 1 in Tilsit

2. Division 3. Infanterie-Brigade Grenadier-Regiment „König Friedrich der Große" (3. Ostpreußisches) Nr. 4 in Rastenburg

2.Division 4.Infanterie-Brigade Füsilier-Regiment „Graf Roon" (Ostpreußisches) Nr. 33 in Gumbinnen

2.Division 3.Infanterie-Brigade Infanterie-Regiment „Graf Dönhoff" (7.Ostpreußisches) Nr. 44 in Goldap

2.Division 4.Infanterie-Brigade 8.Ostpreußisches Infanterie-Regiment Nr. 45 in Insterburg und Darkehmen (1.Bataillon)

2 Division 2 Kavallerie-Brigade Litthauisches Ulanen-Regiment Nr. 12 in Insterburg

2.Division 43.Kavallerie-Brigade Ulanen-Regiment „Graf zu Dohna" (Ostpreußisches) Nr. 8 in Gumbinnen

37.Division 75.Infanterie-Brigade 1. Masurisches Infanterie-Regiment Nr. 146 in Allenstein

37.Division 75.Infanterie-Brigade 1. Ermländisches Infanterie-Regiment Nr. 150 in Allenstein

37.Division 73.Infanterie-Brigade 2. Ermländisches Infanterie-Regiment Nr. 151 in Sensburg und Bischofsburg (2.Bataillon)

37. Division 37. Kavallerie-Brigade Dragoner-Regiment „König Albert von Sachsen" (Ostpreußisches) Nr. 10 in Allenstein

37. Division 37. Kavallerie-Brigade Dragoner-Regiment „von Wedel" (Pommersches) Nr. 11 in Lyck

Pionier-Bataillon „Fürst Radziwill" (Ostpreußisches) Nr. 1 in Königsberg

Samländisches Pionier-Bataillon Nr. 18 in Königsberg

Fußartillerie-Regiment „von Linger" (Ostpreußisches) Nr. 1 in Königsberg

2.Division 2.Feld Artillerie-Brigade Feldartillerie-Regiment „Prinz August von Preußen" (1. Litthauisches) Nr. 1 in Gumbinnen und Insterburg

1 Division 1 Feld Artillerie-Brigade 1. Ostpreußisches Feldartillerie-Regiment Nr. 16 in Königsberg

Ostpreußisches Train-Bataillon Nr. 1 in Königsberg

II ARMEE-KORPS (PREUSSEN)

3. Division in Stettin
4. Division in Bromberg
Jäger-Bataillon „Fürst Bismarck" (Pommersches) Nr. 2 in Kulm
Fußartillerie-Regiment „von Hindersin" (1. Pommersches) Nr. 2 in Swinemünde und Emden
2. Pommersches Fußartillerie-Regiment Nr. 15 in Bromberg und Graudenz
Pommersches Pionier-Bataillon Nr. 2 in Stettin
Pommersche Train-Abteilung Nr. 2 in Altdamm

3 division

5. Infanterie-Brigade in Stettin
  Grenadier-Regiment „König Friedrich Wilhelm IV." (1. Pommersches) Nr. 2 in Stettin
  Colbergsches Grenadier-Regiment „Graf Gneisenau" (2. Pommersches) Nr. 9 in Stargard in Pommern
  Infanterie-Regiment „von der Goltz" (7. Pommersches) Nr. 54 in Kolberg und Köslin (III. Bataillon)
6. Infanterie-Brigade in Stettin
  Füsilier-Regiment „Königin Viktoria von Schweden" (Pommersches) Nr. 34 in Stettin und Swinemünde (III. Bataillon)
  Infanterie-Regiment „Prinz Moritz von Anhalt-Dessau" (5. Pommersches) Nr. 42 in Stralsund und Greifswald (III. Bataillon)
3. Kavallerie-Brigade in Stettin
  Kürassier-Regiment „Königin" (Pommersches) Nr. 2 in Pasewalk
  2. Pommersches Ulanen-Regiment Nr. 9 in Demmin
3. Feldartillerie-Brigade in Stettin
  1. Pommersches Feldartillerie-Regiment Nr. 2 in Kolberg und Belgard (II. Abteilung)
  Vorpommersches Feldartillerie-Regiment Nr. 38 in Stettin

4 division

7. Infanterie-Brigade in Bromberg
  Infanterie-Regiment „Graf Schwerin" (3. Pommersches) Nr. 14 in Bromberg
  6. Westpreußisches Infanterie-Regiment Nr. 149 in Schneidemühl und Deutsch Krone (III. Bataillon)
8. Infanterie-Brigade in Gnesen
  6. Pommersches Infanterie-Regiment Nr. 49 in Gnesen
  4. Westpreußisches Infanterie-Regiment Nr. 140 in Hohensalza
4. Kavallerie-Brigade in Bromberg
  Grenadier-Regiment zu Pferde „Freiherr von Derfflinger" (Neumärkisches) Nr. 3 in Bromberg
  Dragoner-Regiment „von Arnim" (2. Brandenburgisches) Nr. 12 in Gnesen
4. Feldartillerie-Brigade in Bromberg
  2. Pommersches Feldartillerie-Regiment Nr. 17 in Bromberg
  Hinterpommersches Feldartillerie-Regiment Nr. 53 in Bromberg und Hohensalza (I. Abteilung)

3.Division 5.Infanterie-Brigade Grenadier-Regiment „König Friedrich Wilhelm IV." (1. Pommersches) Nr. 2 in Stettin

3.Division 5.Infanterie-Brigade Colbergsches Grenadier-Regiment „Graf Gneisenau" (2.Pommersches) Nr. 9 in Stargard in Pommern

3.Division 6.Infanterie-Brigade Füsilier-Regiment „Königin Viktoria von Schweden" (Pommersches) Nr. 34 in Stettin und Swinemünde

3.Division 6.Infanterie-Brigade Infanterie-Regiment „Prinz Moritz von Anhalt-Dessau" (5. Pommersches) Nr. 42 in Stralsund und Greifswald

3.Division 3.Kavallerie-Brigade Kürassier-Regiment „Königin" (Pommersches) Nr. 2 in Pasewalk

3.Division 3.Kavallerie-Brigade 2.Pommersches Ulanen-Regiment Nr. 9 in Demmin

4.Division 8.Infanterie-Brigade 4. Westpreußisches Infanterie-Regiment Nr. 140 in Hohensalza

4.Division 4.Kavallerie-Brigade Dragoner-Regiment „Baron von Derfflinger" Nr. 3 in Bromberg

4.Division 4.Kavallerie-Brigade Dragoner-Regiment „von Arnim" (2.Brandenburgisches) Nr. 12 in Gnesen

Fußartillerie-Regiment „von Hindersin" (1. Pommersches) Nr. 2 in Swinemünde und Emden

2. Pommersches Fußartillerie-Regiment Nr. 15 in Bromberg und Graudenz

Fußartillerie-Regiment „von Hindersin" (1. Pommersches) Nr. 2 in Swinemünde und Emden

Pommersche Train-Abteilung Nr. 2 in Altdamm

Pommersches Pionier-Bataillon Nr. 2 in Stettin

Jäger-Bataillon „Fürst Bismarck" (Pommersches) Nr. 2 in Kulm

III ARMEE-KORPS (PREUSSEN)

5. Division in Frankfurt (Oder)
6. Division in Brandenburg an der Havel
Landwehr-Inspektion Berlin
Brandenburgisches Jäger-Bataillon Nr. 3 in Lübben
Pionier-Bataillon von Rauch (1. Brandenburgisches) Nr. 3 in Spandau
2. Brandenburgisches Pionier-Bataillon Nr. 28 in Küstrin
Brandenburgische Train-Abteilung Nr. 3
Telegraphen-Bataillon Nr. 2 in Frankfurt und Cottbus

5 division
9. **Infanterie-Brigade** in Frankfurt (Oder)
   Leib-Grenadier-Regiment „König Friedrich Wilhelm III." (1. Brandenburgisches) Nr. 8 in Frankfurt (Oder)
   Infanterie-Regiment „von Stülpnagel" (5. Brandenburgisches) Nr. 48 in Küstrin
10. **Infanterie-Brigade** in Frankfurt (Oder)
    Grenadier-Regiment „Prinz Carl von Preußen" (2. Brandenburgisches) Nr. 12 in Frankfurt (Oder)
    Infanterie-Regiment „von Alvensleben" (6. Brandenburgisches) Nr. 52 in Cottbus und Crossen (I. Bataillon)
5. **Kavallerie-Brigade** in Frankfurt (Oder)
   1. Brandenburgisches Dragoner-Regiment Nr. 2 in Schwedt
   Ulanen-Regiment „Kaiser Alexander II. von Rußland" (1. Brandenburgisches) Nr. 3 in Fürstenwalde
5. **Feldartillerie-Brigade** in Frankfurt (Oder)
   Feldartillerie-Regiment „General-Feldzeugmeister" (2. Brandenburgisches) Nr. 18 in Frankfurt (Oder)
   Neumärkisches Feldartillerie-Regiment Nr. 54 in Küstrin und Landsberg an der Warthe (II. Abteilung)

6 division
11. **Infanterie-Brigade** in Brandenburg an der Havel
    Infanterie-Regiment „Graf Tauentzien von Wittenberg" (3. Brandenburgisches) Nr. 20 in Wittenberg
    Füsilier-Regiment „Prinz Heinrich von Preußen" (Brandenburgisches) Nr. 35 in Brandenburg an der Havel
12. **Infanterie-Brigade** in Brandenburg an der Havel
    Infanterie-Regiment „Großherzog Friedrich Franz II. von Mecklenburg-Schwerin" (4. Brandenburgisches) Nr. 24 in Neuruppin
    Infanterie-Regiment „General-Feldmarschall Prinz Friedrich Karl von Preußen" (8. Brandenburgisches) Nr. 64 in Prenzlau und Angermünde (III. Bataillon)
6. **Kavallerie-Brigade** in Brandenburg an der Havel
   Kürassier-Regiment „Kaiser Nikolaus I. von Russland" (Brandenburgisches) Nr. 6 in Brandenburg an der Havel
   Husaren-Regiment „von Zieten" (Brandenburgisches) Nr. 3 in Rathenow
6. **Feldartillerie-Brigade** in Brandenburg an der Havel
   Feldartillerie-Regiment „General-Feldzeugmeister" (1. Brandenburgisches) Nr. 3 in Brandenburg an der Havel
   Kurmärkisches Feldartillerie-Regiment Nr. 39 in Perleberg
Landwehr-Inspektion Berlin

5.Division 9.Infanterie-Brigade Leib-Grenadier-Regiment „König Friedrich Wilhelm 3" (1.Brandenburgisches) Nr.8 in Frankfurt (Oder)

5. Division 10. Infanterie-Brigade Grenadier-Regiment „Prinz Carl von Preußen" (2. Brandenburgisches) Nr. 12 in Frankfurt (Oder)

5.Division 10.Infanterie-Brigade Infanterie-Regiment „von Alvensleben" (6. Brandenburgisches) Nr. 52 in Cottbus und Crossen

5.Division Feldartillerie-Regiment „General-Feldzeugmeister" (2. Brandenburgisches) Nr. 18 in Frankfurt (Oder)

5.Division 5.Kavallerie-Brigade 1.Brandenburgisches Dragoner-Regiment Nr. 2 in Schwedt

5.Division 5.Kavallerie-Brigade Ulanen-Regiment „Kaiser Alexander 2. von Rußland" (1. Brandenburgisches) Nr. 3 in Fürstenwalde

6.Division 11.Infanterie-Brigade Füsilier-Regiment „Prinz Heinrich von Preußen" (Brandenburgisches) Nr. 35 in Brandenburg an der Havel

6. Division Feldartillerie-Regiment „General-Feldzeugmeister" (1. Brandenburgisches) Nr. 3 in Brandenburg an der Havel

6.Division 6.Kavallerie-Brigade Kürassier-Regiment „Kaiser Nikolaus I. von Russland" (Brandenburgisches) Nr. 6 in Brandenburg an der Havel

6.Division 6.Kavallerie-Brigade Husaren-Regiment „von Zieten" (Brandenburgisches) Nr. 3 in Rathenow

Brandenburgisches Jäger-Bataillon Nr. 3 in Lübben

Pionier-Bataillon von Rauch (1. Brandenburgisches) Nr. 3 in Spandau

Brandenburgische Train-Abteilung Nr. 3

TITOLI PUBBLICATI - ALREADY PUBLISHING

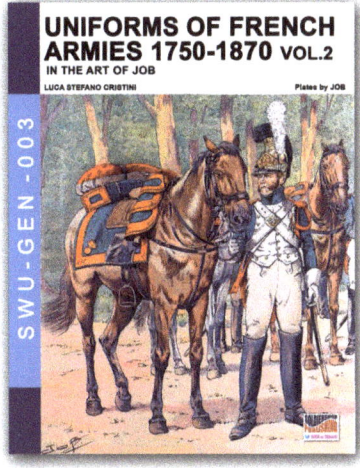
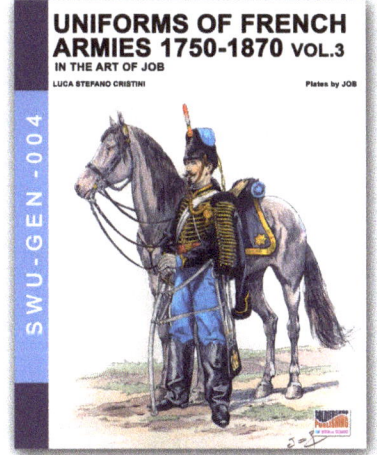
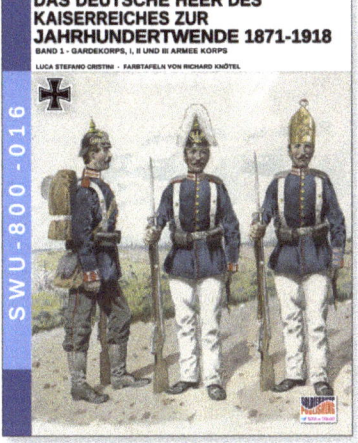

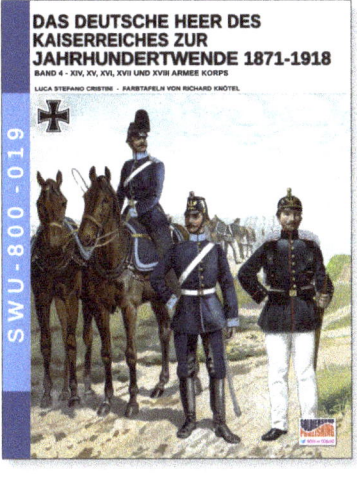

www.ingramcontent.com/pod-product-compliance
Lightning Source LLC
LaVergne TN
LVHW070528070526
838199LV00073B/6723